**Greedy
Cow**

Greedy
Cow

Fiona Sinclair

Smokestack Books
1 Lake Terrace, Grewelthorpe,
Ripon HG4 3BU
e-mail: info@smokestack-books.co.uk
www.smokestack-books.co.uk

ISBN 9781838198879

Smokestack Books
is represented by
Inpress Ltd

Contents

Internet Dating	9
Stood up	10
Bed Snatcher	11
I wanna hold your hand...	12
Not as young as they feel	13
Regeneration	14
Double life	15
Reflex Action	16
A month's trial...	17
Curiosity	18
Small Pool	19
Trying to map you	20
What would you like for Christmas?	22
A changed man	23
A man's woman	24
Locked out	25
Island Weather	26
Night Manoeuvres	27
Warning	28
Out of Step	29
Day Return	30
Sparkler	31
Speechless...	32
Tribute	33
Declassified	34
A period of adjustment	36
Second Wind	37
Rush	38
New Tricks	39
Trust	41
Ménage	42
60th birthday	43
A chorus of disapproval	44
Windfall	45
Still	46

Internet dating

At first my 'best side' photo is mobbed by men
so feel like Scarlett O'Hara at a ball,
until I discover lads seeking carefree cougar sex
or a meal ticket,
and from my own demographic;
inquiries after my hosiery,
and panting mobile numbers.

I search through my matches past Kray twin lookalikes,
married men wearing tell-tale dark glasses,
sad self portraits with bed sit back grounds,
for the handful of guys I might accept a drink from-

beginning to e-flirt with grin and wink emoticons,
over the week I virtual two time
men from Rochester and Deal,
who bus stop chat about work and their tea,
neither making the gear change up to seduction.
Difficult, I suppose, for most blokes
who barely scrawl a birthday card for mum,
to strike a balance between 'Hello Sexy' and 'It's raining here',
and write me into bed with Casanova craft.

Stood Up

Creeping away from bed and favourite thriller,
you must wash your hair, again,
perform yet another make-up legerdemain,
clamp yourself into iron maiden jeans.

At 52, you do not listen for his car's theme tune,
but start to list the weekly shop,
checking clocks you realise he is 30 minutes late,
an old wound's twinge. He has stood you up.

You rehearse a carefree *Where are you?*
to implant in his deaf mobile phone.
Stretch out before *Strictly Come Dancing,*
breaking your diet's indefinite Lent.

Sunday, you find bruising from last night's knock,
not the shame of the mini-jilt ,
but allowing the man's *You have beautiful eyes...*
to turn your middle aged head.

Bed Snatcher

In this room where no man has slept for sixty years,
since grandfather was banished for snoring,
I exchange embroidered lilac for plain blue.

He chuckles at my spinsterish hot water bottle,
companion of an afternoon nap.
Blushing, I fling it to the floor.

His slumberous breathing blares like a brass band.
I need deaf silence to sleep.
Arms and legs advance over the mattress

as I lie watching through the curtain's cleft
for light to agitate the darkness,
cribbed on a ledge of my bed.

I wanna hold your hand...

Second date, hands hibernating in coat pockets,
your elbow is crooked invitingly; I thread my arm through,
our steps synchronise like Fred and Ginger.
By spring, I long for relationship's final consummation,
but blush to make the first move, finally taking
my hand to pull me up steps you do not let go
when my clasp white knuckles yours
on first flight to Crete or my grip clamps you bed side
through eye-watering gynae procedure.

Two years on our real selves' gloves are off,
shopping centre crowds part before your 'Fuck off' face,
But sensing I lack the killer instinct reform before me,
so to maintain hold I must dodge round pensioners,
skip aside pushchairs, breathlessly scattering *Excuse mes.*
Nevertheless, on Whitstable high street I feel damsel protection
as you courtly switch me onto pavement's inside.
At the races preen at my fella looking *like someone off the telly.*
In Turner Contemporary get off on your touch that first seduced me.

Not as young as they feel

After gourmet sex,
they entwine like twins in a womb.
Doze under exhaustion's ether.
Twenty years ago even,
they would be free to slumber until morning.
But, in middle age,
sleep must be prepared for, like a journey,
a check list of pills for pain, cholesterol, blood pressure...
nightclothes, stripped off in present tearing lust,
retrieved from floor and pulled back on,
sheets smoothed, pillows plumped, duvet adjusted,
the final pee.
A *Night Night* kiss,
then easing onto back and side,
the width of a double bed growing between them.

Regeneration

In his mum's spare room, a paper bag leaking photos.
Your fingers ache to scrabble amongst its contents for
the small boy with the *Just William* schemes,
the glam rocker dating two girls simultaneously,
the buccaneering biker always outwitting the bill...
Instead your faux casual *I've found some old pictures.*

On the sofa, he hoards the photos in his lap,
examines each snap with jeweller's glass scrutiny,
leaving you sweating until he metes them out.
Dead father and step-mother are given faces now,
but you find that his face is often missing
from holidays at Pontins and family knees ups,
away on another pin in the map of the world, adventure –

Flashes of bouffant white dress and formal suit,
the room takes an in breath *Do you want to see these?*
The bravado of your *I'd like to...*
Signing the register, arm in arm outside the church,
with slicked back mullet and Zapata moustache,
features that drink has begun to lay waste,
Georgie Best lost boy look in the eyes,
You wouldn't pick him out in a police line-up...

Your man, nearly losing limbs not to a daredevil
bike crash but arteries clogged like the M25,
exorcised the booze and fags,
won back the title of 'big brother'
the clever mathematician
with solutions to his siblings problems,
who tends his hair like a lawn,
is quite the dandy in Crombie and brogues.
So you are marrying a regenerated Dr Who

Double life

Best suit he ever owned?
Bespoke; inky velvet, large lapels, fitted flares.
Him and his mate shopping for
white ruffled blue dress shirt to complement.
Collar secured by midnight velvet tie.
Whole outfit topped off with 4-inch black stacks.
Show stopper entering night clubs,
peacock strutting over to buy a girl a drink,
them stroking his coney soft shoulder length hair
as he Jagger charmed them.

But a weekend glam rocker only.
Weekdays, buckled biker boots that domino toppled
row of Vespas on Margate sea front,
'must have' Kangol helmet,
full visor slapped down like a knight into battle,
surcoat, a cut down jean jacket,
emblazoned with his personal coat of arms;
Invicta horse rampant for Kentish boy,
all four aces pictured in card sharp warning
above metal studded nick name 'Maverick'.

Reflex Action

Mannequin thin, she studies the menu outside,
you ruche your top over a proved stomach,
return your gaze to his face
in time to catch the reflexive flick of his eyes
up and down the woman's body,
whilst still yarning about 'childhood Whitstable'.
Jolt like a small electric shock as,
for a split second, he is a stranger
who took his pick of biker birds,
whistled strippers on friend's charity stag nights,
slipped like Flash Harry into that local newsagent
for under the counter mags.
No point now chilling the cappuccino and hot chocolate
by attempting a laddish 'I saw you looking'
because you know he would not recall seeing her...

A month's trial...

Attempting to butch up your girly home,
you consign Marilyn cushions to the spare room,
replace boudoir duvets with dark covers.
Underwear entwining in a 'big wash',
your vegetarian trolley re-discovers
the meat counter at Tesco's.
His 'You're trying too hard'
is drowned out by the vacuum cleaner.

But after years of solitary living,
you long to replace your siren shift
with comfy leggings and Tee shirt,
stretching out in your bed like a cat before a fire.
Read a chapter on the loo,
encouraging your coy bowels to poo
without anxious 'Are you alright? 'up the stairs.

And when he blames village water for his unruly hair,
mock winces at your cheese grater towels,
will not exchange constitutional beach walk for bridle paths;
it becomes clear that you are some way off
handing in sea view keys
and adding his name to your rent book.

Curiosity

Driven by the Iago voice in your head
you let yourself into his Google account,
rifle through in box, trash, spam...
until you find an email that scorches your fingers.

Brandishing his billet doux like lipstick on a collar,
Your 'Can't you see how I feel?'
Is met with a bewildered child's gaze
'but the words mean nothing'.
So he talks you round with 'the only woman for me...'
but his good night email becomes 'Blah, blah, blah'
that is skim read then trashed.

Compelled by friends choric 'But he lied',
you unlock his phone with fumbling fingers.
One contact blazes like a red neon sign,
pointing to a website that punches you in the face.

You send his belongings packing to the shed,
but his email, 'everyone has a past'
gets his foot back in the door of your life.
Still, watching TV, teaching grammar, buying clothes –
You self-harm by envisaging:
his Vauxhall joining other cars in a dark layby,
NSA stilettos tripping up to his flat,
him meeting a broadminded couple for coffee....

Small Pool

Swimming in slow dance tempo,
they gaze at each other with sugar rush eyes,
chattering about A Levels, Saturday jobs...

At their age, whilst your leather coated biker chicks balanced
with cat woman cool on the back of your Norton,
I was a Laura Ashley girl,
who only had eyes for Kings School Boys.

Now, as you enjoy the water with otter zeal,
I attempt a gasping breast stroke,
trying to keep my make-up intact,
on this our first holiday since Aunty Internet fixed us up.

Trying to map you

I was a debt collector once: usual static shock
at some new revelation about your past,
a politician's deflection to my *When was this*?
So more details I can't place on your Jackson Pollock time-line.
Over a year you have wooed me with
ripping yarns of life as an engineer overseas:
rock star strutting onto Concorde twice,
commuting to work on a camel in a sandstorm,
the gilded cage of 5 star hotels from weeks to months.
Then, lottery win salaries in your pocket,
de-mob happy, no contest for you and your mate
between the UK or sticking a pin in an atlas.
Back home, between contracts, you took
the covers off the Ducati, Norton, Triumph,
one finger to plods as you G-forced up the motorway
to your side-line turning Shepherd Neame pubs around
with clenched fists, a head for maths, Barnum ingenuity.
One vacation, you work a tramp steamer
through the back door into Australia,
police cells like an over-night stay in B and B,
steak and beers for dinner, when a visa releases you,
another of your chance meetings, chatting to a man in a bar,
who has just lost a British engineer, you stay three years...

Decades wielding tools heavy as training weights takes its toll,
a *hope I die before I get old* attitude means no savings at 50,
but your canny agent reveals a modest pension
you supplement by ducking and weaving about Sussex...
Your constant first-person narrative infers
only man's best friend for company now,
but once, post coitus, you disclose *Oh no I was living with*
Showing me photos of bespoke doll's houses,
you let slip this hobby started as a labour of love for...
Sometimes the 'I' does mean living alone,
sharing Christmas Dinner with two blokes from the pub.
Trouble is, when our relationship first began to close in on my
own back-ground, my gambled *Let's not talk about the past*,
was accepted by you with poker player cool.
Over time, as my secrets burst their locks,
I expected us to both show our hands,
but you grip onto our contract like a winning betting slip.

What would you like for Christmas?

Your little boy lament *Surprise me. I never get surprises.*
Months searching the high street for
Jones brogues, Ted Baker sweaters, Calvin Klein cologne...

You prefer to internet shop from sofa watching Channel 4 racing,
Write me a list; I'd rather get you something you want.
Tell-tale ads on my Google page reveal months
drooling over sparkly earrings, fancy pens, shiny stilettos...
Just one would satisfy my glittery craving,
but rejection slip slap when I realise *Not value for money*
isn't a tease.

You begin to plant parcels under the tree until
I'm a bit disappointed with your main present...
Do you want to see it now?
Groping for glasses, I peer at atom sized studs
that apparently looked bigger in the eBay photo,
Refund in hand, you take on Christmas Eve crowds,
Jewellers' names sown like hypnotist's triggers,
at your *Well I've paid more than I wanted,* my hopes lark soar...

Christmas morning, the slow strip tease
of unwrapping your thoughtful:
bird table for my sofa twitching,
page markers for my readings,
heart throb poster for my Dickens' crush,
climaxes in the final parcel's sexy promise,
whose clothes I rip off to reveal – Turkish Delight,
summer holiday remembrance,
I go off to baste the goose wearing nothing dazzling
instead a child's disappointment.

A changed man

First sight, you are sober coat, cable knit sweater and slacks,
then in the café a gold chocker chain works out above your collar,
past it as 80s rolled up jacket sleeves and mullet, a bogey turn-off for me.

Months later tucking your shirt in tent peg tight, my faux casual,
Have you tried wearing it outside your jeans?
Later at the party nibbling at small talk and nuts your hissed *I feel scruffy.*

The Crombie is spotted in a TV drama, horse cheering excitement
as you scan for it in every scene. I buy one for Christmas, awaken your
sleeping dandy as you fuss with silk pocket handkerchief, buy aviator
                                                                    sunglasses.

Coat's first outing, clitoral appreciation as I watch your peacock strut,
catching other men admiring it, you order two more for *every-day,*
the mail order catalogue for men of a certain age, binned now.

That birthday, you lose years as I upgrade economy Tesco shoes, Pound Land
scent, to my business class Clarks brogues, Calvin Klein cologne.
In breath at sight of you in the Ted Baker waist coat worn to surprise gig.

A good Cheltenham means premium M & S jackets elbow Asda counterparts
out of your wardrobe, drawers prove with Burton's v necks, red and purple
replacing beige and brown; wearing them I notice your throat is free now of
the chain, a gift from siblings bought with pocket money you
swore never to divest, whose breakage I inwardly punched the air
at, that is still waiting to be repaired, my only worry that they
think I made you take it off...

A man's woman

Lulled by her 'Plain Jane' months,
I'm shunt shocked – she has slimmed down
to her flirting weight,
whereas I am still dragging Christmas around.
kiss-kiss *You smell nice* to my fella holding the car door open.
Getting drinks in whilst he bags seats,
she suggests a tribute band the following week,
not his thing but I'm game.
My back turned to greet acquaintance,
she ignores girls' night out rules
burlesque teases her big hair,
whilst issuing a personal invitation he can't refuse.

Years myself being odd woman out,
I insist she sits between us,
become gooseberry as they chatter
about mutual Australian experience.
Despite my knowing he scores:
too poor, too old... on her mate check list,
tonight, amidst other middle-aged men
who have standard slid into Tees and trainers,
He scrubs up well in Crombie, Ted Baker scarf, Brogues.
Although other girlfriends dismiss her,
I know whilst women prize Audrey and Marilyn,
men salivate over Stevie Nicks and the *sexy one from Abba.*
So when her sapphire eyes briefly meet mine and smirk,
my laughter at the comedian on stage curdles,
as once again I wonder what her game is...

Locked out

Sometimes you are a sealed strong box with no spare key.
I strive to jemmy you with chisel questions – but scrape my skin,
struggle to unpick you with hair pin chatter – but prick my fingers,
smarting I watch TV, listen for your combination click, *Can I get
you anything?*

Island Weather

When his small boy self visits,
I want to kiss eyes that reboot to childhood settings,
ruffle hair that reverts to a kid's quiff,
But this child is skittish as a spirit guide
So I must sit on my hands whilst he recounts
multiple paper rounds to fund bicycle.

Then the hood moves in,
machine gun firing 'Fucks' at elderly drivers, jaywalkers...
stabbing his keyboard in a web chat with some bookie.
These times I glimpse the teenage biker rucking on Margate Beach,
the man whose drinking years were tinder to this temper,
hide in silence until the reassuring touch on my knee...

Sometimes the dodgy geezer,
calculator brain reckoning the odds on *not getting caught,*
whose plan to *risk it* I initially agree to....
But putting my home on the table is too high a stake,
unable to swat away my *What Ifs,*
he presents a bouquet of official forms.

Always the old school gent,
greeting men with a hand shake, women with a peck.
Notes slipped into a pocket, *Pay it back when you can.*
strangers the beneficiary of his directions, a lift...
And when my fault line brain triggers another earth quake
he holds me firmly *I'm here,* till my world stops rocking.

Night Manoeuvres

Making my bedside choice that first night,
we still start each slumber spooning to the left.

Anaconda arm wrapped around my waist, you plunge
straight into sleep, but some nights valium fails me,

stiff limbs yearn to shift, I squirm sweat slicked onto my back,
fantasise nights in spare bed, snow angel stretch on cool white sheets...

Second you shift, I claim the space with right side foetal,
default single years stance that acts like hypnotic suggestion.

Early hours you have emigrated to the divan's far side, mountainous
back cold shoulders, no attempt to cross the desert lonely bed between us,

Dawn, you knock on my dreams smoothing bum and breasts,
not serious seduction but an erotic dream's virtual foreplay.

At 7am my stomach's alarm call; unable to synchronise our waking,
I watch the clock hand's slow scale to 8, when you begin to surface,

etiquette established weekends at your flat, where I lay lulled by
your ebb and flow breath until 'Careful it's hot'. Best porridge ever.

Now full time in my house: I put kettle on, open curtains, de-frost steak,
trek back upstairs bearing your breakfast of full-bodied tea.

Warning

Perhaps it is my constant cat walk,
that makes you remember, *'I've always fancied a Crombie.'*
When the on-course bookie nods 'Nice coat mate'
you accessorize with a strut
that recalls the youth who bought black velvet suit
and stacks for nights out in Margate,
white linen three piece for Monte Carlo,
dinner dress bespoke for Arab feasts...

Sherpa knowing the lie of Matalan,
I sabotage our trip for dinner service,
strategically losing us in menswear,
'Those are sexy' to passing V necks
You buy three in 'Look at me colours'.
Birthday kick-off catalogue slip-ons
easing into my gift of high street brogues.

Soon a south London gang of Crombies
Mobs my coats in the wardrobe,
Now in between computing odds
you calculate: imperial purple silk handkerchief
with black coat, scarlet with grey,
macho enough to carry off
matching gloves and stud in pocket.

Now in Whitstable High street *Are you off the telly*?
puffs out your chest in pukkah waistcoat.
Neighbour devours your words
about boundary business with crimson mouth,
cold shouldering me with back turned,
afterwards *'Did you see her flirting*?'
But I have not abetted you stripping off 10 years
with every functional jacket and Christmas sweater
for some other woman to become the beneficiary.

Out of Step

Occasionally now my Canterbury amble
does not keep time with your south London strut,
so I must adjust my steps to yours...

Day Return

Breakfasting alone as you're on a Jolly Boys outing,
I take up again with my old chum radio 4.
Too early in the marriage to consider this time to myself a treat,
rather it recalls years of matinees avoiding 'odd woman out' stares.
Finding myself the only single at weddings, dinners...
wanting to floor the car home to bed and chocolate,
instead dragging on my *I don't Care* motley.
Understanding that Christmas, Easter, Bank Holidays
families closed the circle to outsiders.
So binged on TV, Old films, vodka...

She values her independence,
friends writing me a 'Tatler' life,
but my social whirl was Bluewater every Saturday.
Too proud to confess, I wanted a man beside me.
Then you pitch up; belated for kids playing in the garden,
nevertheless filling the house with your gentleman's paraphernalia,
my diary with family dos, race meets, rock concerts.
So returning home to pot luck dinner for one,
I lie in bed listening over the' you substitute' telly, for your key,
until *Hallo, Hallo* up the stairs, and I smile.

Sparkler

Espresso high on his proposal,
no thoughts of a ring until on the Ponte Vecchio
amidst the blaze of bling,
his disappointment at the Medici price tags.
Time was I could have let you loose with my credit card.
You had sworn off real jewellery anyway,
after watching mother milk men for sapphires, diamonds...
Found yourself drawn to modest silver and faux-pearl.
Your friends will think I'm a cheapskate
But this ring would always mean;
hot chocolate he stood a spoon up in,
your OMG at the scale of 'David'.
the Duomo photo-bombing every view.

Designer bags raised friends' expectations,
your extended hand met with a pause,
'It's very you', 'How unusual'
the backstory beginning to sound an excuse.
Handling his heart like cutting a precious gem
you obtain his blessing to buy something glittery,
a We'll see to your paying for it yourself.
He sacrifices the meet at Sandown to ring shop,
but you soon find emeralds don't come cheap.
In the 11th hour jewellers, *I'd forgotten about this one,*
two diamond body guards flanking a superstar stone,
old stock at pre-goldrush prices,
knocked into your price range
by his cheeky chappy *How much for cash*?
In the car you take it from its conker casing,
you and the ring both off the shelf now.

Speechless...

Stepping into 'the dress' her aunt barges in,
'What do you think of my new jacket?'
She pauses in wedding undies to praise detailing...
satisfied her aunt whisks off to paparazzi loiter in the living room.
Toddler stepping downstairs in high heels baring bouquet.
She is movie star needy today for 'You look lovely'.
Instead, her aunt picks up some village gossip's thread,
as if she was in leggings and Tee.
When the photo call is a couple of snaps,
'Any minute now' in her head begins to die.
Two friends arrive to squire her to the ceremony,
her aunt bustles off to work with ordinary day 'Bye'
she strains for 'Good Luck' until the front door slams.
In the motor to the registry ached belief
'I have failed to find the wow factor for him'.
But in the car park, he beams 'you look stunning',
suddenly she is red carpet glamour
in the scarlet prom dress, his favourite colour.
Later, in photos, she sees the something borrowed
that day was her mother's beauty,
wonders if the old Hollywood hair, make up, smile
reminded her aunt of the dead sister,
still unforgiven for her good looks...

Tribute

Seville sight-seeing in 40 degrees stokes up fever heat in me.
Leant arms sweat slew off table as if tipsy.
Folded legs slide apart as if 1950's gran on Margate sea front.
Bottom sticks to seat as if sitting on drying paint.

White deflects heat I learn from chic Sevillian women,
Q tip thin in linen shifts; they cat walk the city.
But after six months dieting to make the wedding dress weight,
I have honeymoon troughed on tapas, artisan ice cream, paella,
growing a 2nd trimester belly in 3 weeks that old ladies smile and pat.
So I sit in the café in emergency purchase dress whose loose
folds do not camouflage but balloon me to morbidly obese.

She is Spanish siesta fresh, sleeveless dress skims a trim body
middle age has not troubled with 'problem areas'.
Her partner, returning from the bar, drops a kiss on her neck's nape,
not the lust of breast or bum fondle,
but spontaneous reminder she is adored,
which the woman accepts with a private message smile.
Envy prickles as I dig into my chocolate pudding.

Declassified

Saturday evening, we imbibe nostalgia,
watching vintage *Top of the Pops*, where bands with
gender shifting costumes and up to mischief kohled eyes,
evoke *Oh I remember them*. Suddenly a secret,
kept from your late mum all these years, is declassified.

Bike shed, between drags, you boys chewed over
Radio Caroline's announcement; UK's own Woodstock
with a fantasy rock line up. Their choric *Oh, Fuck*
at being indentured to mock O Levels. But you,
under cover of a *weekend camping with a mate*,
left cramming school chums and trained it to Portsmouth.
Handicapped by looking more ten than teenager,
you outwitted *no unaccompanied minor*s on ferry
by tagging onto a Brady Bunch family off to Butlins,
whilst you, boy scout prepared with tinned food, primus, tent,
made your way to the 1970 Isle of Wight Rock festival.

I shake my head as yet another priceless memory is unlocked
from your past's safety deposit box.
My teenage years tethered to mum, I am greedy for details.
Only one stage so acts Lilliputian figures,
but a battalion of Marshall amps boomed around the field,
where makeshift tents were thrown up like a refugee camp.
The Who, The Move, T Rex...
And then, you hold up your memory's Star of India,
Hendrix of course. Early hours of the morning,
trademark purple hat, flower power shirt, hussar waistcoat,
making the other bands look bottom of the bill,
just days off joining the 27 club.
So, whilst the rest of us can only goggle at grainy TV footage,
you bear witness that his playing *was something else*.

At the festival, you worked out your life's equation;
(desire + action + luck) = adventure.
Two years on with A Levels stuffed in your back pocket,
passed prodigy early, you sloughed off school,
leaving mates who had parked their dreams with a sigh,
still swotting towards jobs in banks, civil service, sales.

A period of adjustment

Initially, you only physically move into this house,
where Nana's embossed wallpaper still manifests,
despite my many paint jobs. Her riotous carpets resisting
my efforts to sedate with plain rugs, whilst the garden,
without her firm hand, frowns in at the windows.

Together we restrain rowdy shrubs, see off feral weeds,
take a chainsaw to anarchic trees. Inside, set about evicting
her décor. I inwardly grimace at your choice of purple wallpaper,
whilst assuring *No I like it,* but pasting as you hang,
conceded it as stately rather than sombre,

especially when augmented by a spanking new amethyst carpet.
And my mini chandeliers you thought OTT camp
are permitted to stay, now you see them in context.
Allocating a wall each for paintings: your stable of Stubbs
co-exists with my bevy of pre-Raphaelites.

Our brainwave for the stairs, a Rock's hall of fame,
shared sport of tracking down classic albums on eBay,
my *Sticky fingers*; your *Billion Dollar Baby.*
And crowning the stair well, our Liverpool FC
This is Anfield sign; that we touch each day for luck.

Second Wind

Retiring at 65, you get a second wind.
Your mornings are tinkering.
Your afternoons are feet up watching classic 90's TV.
At Aintree, your black Crombie with a flash of red shirt
draws *You look cool man* tributes from booted and suited lads,
and your trademark hair, splendid as a crest,
has older men, smoothing bald-pates and sighing *Nice cut mate*.

At 59, I am winded by five months repeating revision litany
to private pupils at vespers hour,
bingeing in the car on Snickers for sugar spike to keep my eyes open.
Carrying my weight gain with the shame of a 1950's unmarried mother.

At the Grand National, all I can throw together
is beige shift dress, dun coat, grey hat,
a pheasant hen's dowdy plumage.

Whilst you glide on the current of such compliments,
I flap behind, trying with clipped-wing confidence
to keep up with you.

Rush

Mid-winter morning I lug bloated bags through the door,
still frowning from encounters with mums and their toddlers,
unruly as puppies, to be greeted by 'Shouldn't have left me alone',
your laptop displaying a motorcycle for sale whose retro looks
stirs memories of past bike loves, and 'is a steal'.
Suddenly, all previous tutting at middle aged men
on bikes 'They can't handle', mutterings of
'Trying to recapture their youth' are forgotten.
Replaced now by 'It will help my back', 'Get me exercising'.
But I have known by the way you ogle bikes in car parks,
this is an itch you must scratch.

By Friday it is parked outside.
First fine day you armour up in a leather jacket
reinforced like a knight's brigandine,
select a private road at the rear of the house
to get to grips with: 'wing mirrors all wrong',
'brakes on the wrong side'.
I tip toe up the path, peep through a crack in the fence
as you go through the protocol of 'lid' on, then Raybans,
under which disguise, you time travel back to your 20s.
You mount, and after decades out of the saddle,
roar off down the road with Steve McQueen cool,

leaving me behind. And jealousy abrades
at this old passion rekindled,
as if I have reluctantly agreed to an infidelity,
because I have nothing comparable in my past
to give me this *Woo Hoo*! high.
Dancing once, perhaps, but not now with my disobedient body.
Suddenly, I understand why those Whitstable women
don wet suits and take to wild swimming with *whoops*,
rather than seek their thrills amongst the WI.
I retrace down the path, noting the garden chores
that are pending, to coffee and online solitaire.

New Tricks

The hat and dress I fussed to find for 60th
birthday bash remains box bound. Instead,
I am kitted out with biker armour,
donning the dead weight jacket with a grunt,
all fingers and thumbs with the helmet.
But, *I won't take you out until:*
you get the measure of the machine,
become road savvy for local ruts and drain covers
that might unseat; feels like a reprieve,
suspecting that your fantasy of me as pillion will fizzle.

Not for you refresher lessons, but a *once a biker*
faith that it will all come back to you,
as if riding was an autonomic function,
and for several weeks its, *I'm off on the bike* with reports
back in tones giddy as rekindling an old love affair,
then suddenly, *I can take you out now.*
First ride, I hide beneath my helmet, the *Let's get it over with*
expression, usually reserved for facing, without flinching,
monster credit card bills, mammograms ...

My 60 year-old legs struggle to develop over the seat
that I must perch upon, no bigger than a bar stool.
For now, I have permission to place my arms
around you but generally you dislike it,
since it feels more boa constrictor than sexy biker chick embrace.
As the bike moves off, the winter pitted roads wind me
so that my body screams for a seat belt,
first encounters with buses, HGVs,
I mentally crouch, missing a car's metal carapace.

Once on the by-pass you accelerate, the velocity
hurricane buffets me, but simultaneously,
my own driver's instincts kick in as I peer over
your shoulder, scanning for on-coming jeopardy.
The first corners present like the fairground rides
I have always avoided, my instinct is to pull against the tilt
in self-preservation, fortunately you are experienced
enough to compensate for my wrestle with gravity.

But there is a moment, up Courtney road, where
the road's camber is air strip smooth,
and the woods seem to keep pace like running children.
I notice donkeys in a field, a coy cottage hidden behind hedges,
details overlooked in my car as, music blaring,
I bowl through the present, eyes fixed on the road ahead.
Back home I am fizzing, and receiving your blue riband
praise *I didn't even know you were there*,
swagger up the garden path.

Trust

You must trust him, he knows what he is doing.
So I wrench my eyes from on-coming cars,
avert my gaze as buses scrape past us,
look at the sky whilst you negotiate doddery cycle riders,
allowing you to lead me in this riotous quick step.
Until, an argy bargy with white vans on roundabouts,
I simply smile and shrug *He'll sort it,*
giggle as at traffic lights we weave past stationary
four-wheel drives, as if waved through like VIPs.
Follow his shoulder line on corners and, at first, I talk myself
through each curve as if to a nervous child,
but over time given the *snakey or dual carriage way* option,
I chose the Herne Bay twists that over the weeks
we take lower and faster like our personal TT.
And sometimes we blast up the M2 doing a ton,
wind rattling my lid, battering my jacket,
in the wing mirrors, grinning at each other in cahoots.

Ménage

She has a retro glamour. Your *What do you think of her?*
is deaf to my response, and *Shall we go and have a look?*
rhetorical, so I know that I have competition on my hands.

To be fair, you say that you won't purchase unless I ride pillion.
As a teenager I was warned against rough biker boys who were
as dangerous as their machines, so have never even sat on a bike.

So you construct a mock-up with stool, chair, sofa arm; instruct me in
the protocol of mounting. I sit astride. *Would you feel comfortable on that?*
I nod, forgetting that this cycle simulator is not moving at 80mph.

You joke about joining gentlemen of a certain age, previously
tutted at for trying to recapture their youth on thoroughbred bikes
they don't know how to handle. Now, you buy T shirts with slogans,

complicit in the lark of old bikers returning to the saddle.
And just as I followed you onto planes to daredevil destinations,
friends purse their lips as you get me, at 60, on the back of this bike,

and from the off, what was meant to be your affair becomes a ménage,
as I watch the weekly weather report for the next fine days,
and our holidays hijacked, we hop on the bike and race out of lock down.

60th birthday

Our diaries are torn up that March.
Your internet searches to find some way to mark
my 60th are all dead ends.
But, in the two months since you got the motorbike,
I have learned to take corners so low I could tag the tarmac,
compensate for shunts at junctions and lights
by leaning back against the *sissy bar*,
adjust my position when pot-holes wind, with a wriggle,
even chat at raucous night club volume, as we motor along.
So, I decide a blast down to Margate,
for chips and ice cream on the seafront, is gift enough,
because your coaxing me at 60,
on the back of a motor bike, is the new adventure,
every bit as exotic as my eyes scaling
the great pyramids, and still part of you,
pivoting my life 360 degrees.

A chorus of disapproval

Friends shake their heads, take in breaths,
Well you'd never get me on the back of one,
shuddered anecdotes of broken bodies and worse.

Same tuts as when we chose to holiday in Istanbul,
over Ithaka, *Have you got a death wish?*
As if bombs went off as regularly as Adhams.

But this year has reminded me how catastrophe can
career around the corner and collide head on
with the most demur of lives.

So, always wearing bikers' full armour, we cruise
off down to Margate, for ice cream on the sea wall,
then back intime for Father Brown on the telly.

Although I confess that on curfew quiet country roads
I dare myself to outstretch arms, then squeal as you join me,
and we motor along in bird flight simulation.